Hope this is fun, dear Ivy!

Mix and Match Recipes

Your pal,

Rosanna

For multiple sales or group discounts contact Champion Press, Ltd., PMB 329, 8689 North Port Washington Road, Milwaukee, WI 53217
www.championpress.com

Mix and Match Recipes

Creative Ideas for Busy Kitchens
Deborah Taylor-Hough

CHAMPION PRESS LTD.

Milwaukee, Wisconsin

Other books by Deborah Taylor-Hough

FROZEN ASSETS: HOW TO COOK FOR A DAY
   AND EAT FOR A MONTH
FROZEN ASSETS LITE & EASY
A SIMPLE CHOICE: A PRACTICAL GUIDE FOR SAVING
   YOUR TIME, MONEY AND SANITY
CURRICULUM YELLOW PAGES

Audio Cassettes by Deborah Taylor-Hough
COOKING FOR THE FREEZER
LIVING WITHIN YOUR MEANS

Table of Contents

Introduction

"What's for dinner, Mom?"

Ever hear that question in your house? I think I hear it nearly every day of the week ... and at least half a dozen times on weekends.

But sometimes the cupboard's bare and time is severely limited. It's hard to answer that dinner question then. Ever been there? I know I have. Even one of those situations—hungry kids, empty shelves, or no time—can add up to another trip through the local drive-thru or a quick call to the pizza delivery guy. And if you add tight finances into the equation, it's pretty much impossible to order fast food, or even run out to the store for last-minute ingredients to prepare some new gourmet recipe from your favorite magazine.

On those "Old Mother Hubbard days" when the troops are clamoring for something more nourishing than dry spaghetti noodles straight from the package, wouldn't it be great to transform that lonely can of stewed tomatoes, a stray packet of chicken soup mix, a few partially emptied pasta boxes, and some frozen mixed veggies into something tasty for the family?

Well, welcome to my world—the world of *Mix and Match Recipes*. Making a "real" meal out of assorted odds and ends from the pantry and refrigerator? Is it possible? Is it even edible? You bet it is!

In one of Rosamunde Pilcher's books, she says, "Happiness is making the most of what you have." Not only is that a good motto to live by, it's also an accurate description of the philosophy behind this book's collection of recipes. The concept of Mix and Match recipes is making the most of what you have: in your pantry, refrigerator and freezer.

No more last minute trips to the store. No more panic about what to eat when you run out of money before you run out of month. As long as you can unearth a few dusty cans on a shelf somewhere, there's a good chance a Mix and Match meal awaits. These recipe ideas cover the entire gamut of eating ... soups, appetizers, desserts, main meals, snacks. If you can name it, you can probably Mix and Match it!

The recipes in this book are the result of creatively meeting the needs and desires of my family over many years of living on a tight budget with competing demands on my time and energy. Sounds a bit like the story of modern American life, doesn't it? Extremely busy, sometimes broke, but always resilient and resourceful.

Not all of the experiments on our family's way to Mix and Match heaven were a success—but just the process itself was always a lot of fun. Even my three kids learned to enjoy making their own Mix and Match soups and skillet meals. Never knowing how the final product would turn out was half the fun—a true adventure in eating. Remember that old children's story about Stone Soup? Everyone came along and threw a little of this and a little of that into the pot with the stone, and before their eyes, the first unofficial Mix and Match soup was born! And remember how much they all loved it? I've learned that contributing to the final product goes a long way toward increasing a child's enjoyment of their meal.

Just think of Mix and Match cooking as an art form all its own. I'll give you the general guidelines and starting points—you take it from there and see what tasty concoctions your kitchen has hiding in the dark recesses of its shelves and drawers.

To get started using this book, you won't need to run out to the store and stock up on hard to find ingredients. Just pick from what you already have on hand. You'll also find some simple recipes and ideas that encourage fun—like make-it-yourself spa treatments, and some easy recipes and crafts for kids.

I wish you many years of happy cooking in your own busy—and creative—kitchen.

Deborah Taylor-Hough
May 2002

Mix and Match Soup
(8 generous servings)

Base of Broth...Choose One

Tomato: One 12-oz. can tomato paste PLUS two 16-oz. cans tomatoes with juice (chopped) PLUS water to equal 10 cups total.

Chicken/Turkey: 10 cups broth *or* 4 bouillon cubes dissolved in 10 cups water.

Beef: 10 cups broth *or* 4 bouillon cubes dissolved in 10 cups water.

Protein...
Choose One (1 lb.or 2 cups, cooked)

Ground beef, browned
Leftover meatballs or meatloaf, chopped
Cooked chicken or turkey, cut up Ham, cut up
Lentils (raw)
Frankfurters, sliced (any sausage or Kielbasa)
Pepperoni, sliced
Cooked dry beans (pintos, kidney,
Great Northern, garbanzos, or a
mixture of whatever is on hand)

Grain...Choose One or Two
(2 cups)

Rice, cooked (any variety)
Barley, cooked
Pasta, raw
Corn
Dumplings (add at end of cooking time)

Vegetables...Choose Two or More
(1-2 cups sliced, diced or shredded)

Carrots
Celery

Cabbage
Onion
Potatoes
Tomatoes
Green Beans
Yellow "Wax" Beans
Turnips
Parsnips

Potatoes
Broccoli
Peas or pea pods
Cauliflower
Green Pepper
Zucchini
Corn

Seasonings...
Choose 2-4 (1-2 teaspoons each)

Basil
Cayenne (dash)
Chives
Cumin
Garlic
Marjoram

Onion powder
Thyme
Rosemary
Parsley
Oregano

To Prepare Soup:

Bring stock to boil in large stock pot or Dutch oven. Add all ingredients; salt and pepper to taste; reduce heat; simmer one hour.

Crockpot Prep:

Pour boiling stock and other ingredients into crock pot and simmer 8 - 12 hours or overnight on LOW setting.

Pasta Presto

(6 servings)

Choose 8 ounces
of one of the following:

Vermicelli
Fettuccini
Angel Hair Pasta
Spaghetti
Egg Noodles

Choose one of the following:

6 slices turkey bacon, cut into ½ to 1 inch pieces
¾ cup ham, cubed
½ pound ground beef
½ pound steak, cut into pieces
½ pound chicken breasts, cut into pieces

Choose one of the following:

1 cup frozen peas
1 cup broccoli florets
1 cup French style green beans

You may also wish to add
6 green onions, sliced thinly

Ready, Set, Cook...

Cook pasta as directed on box and drain. In a skillet, cook meat of choice until crisp or browned. Add one jar of light-alfredo sauce. Stir in noodles and vegetables. Cook for 10-15 minutes or until heated through and vegetables are crisp-tender.

Create a Casserole
(6 servings)

Choose one food from each of the following categories...unless otherwise noted

Protein...1 lb. or 1 ½ cups cooked

Tuna (1 can)
Ground beef, pork or turkey
Ham, cut up
Eggs, hard-cooked and chopped
Chopped beef, pork or ham
Chicken or turkey, cut up
Fish, cooked and cut up
Frankfurters, sausage, or Kielbasa, cooked and cut up

Vegetables...1-½ to 2 cups canned, cooked or raw

Green beans
Peas
Asparagus
Spinach
Mixed vegetables
Corn
Any other vegetables of your choosing

Breads & Cereals...1 cup, raw

Spaghetti
Macaroni
Potatoes, sliced or cubed
Pasta (any)
Rice (white or brown)
Bulgar
Millet
Quick Barley

Sauce...1 can soup plus 1-½ same-soup-size cans of milk, or water...or 2 cups sauce

Cream of Potato, Chicken, Celery, Asparagus or
Mushroom Soup
Tomato Soup
French Onion Soup
White sauce (homemade)
Sour cream
Stewed tomatoes, undrained plus one can water or broth

Extras...choose one or two, up to 1 cup total

Pimento
Almonds, sliced or slivered
Green chilies, chopped
Envelope taco seasoning mix

Topping, 1 cup

Potato chips or round buttery
crackers, crushed
Yellow Cheese (any), grated
Monterey Jack, grated
Mozzarella, grated
Stuffing mix or breadcrumbs
Parmesan cheese

We're cooking now....

Choose one food from each of the groups above. Thoroughly mix your choice of above ingredients (except topping). Season to taste with salt, pepper, soy sauce, onion flakes, garlic or any spices you enjoy. If mixture seems dry, add ½ cup milk, water or stock. Place in buttered casserole dish; sprinkle on choice of topping. Bake uncovered at 350 F for 1 hour.

A Plethora of Pops

FUDGE POPS: Prepare instant chocolate pudding according to package directions. Pour into pop molds. Freeze.

ROCKY ROAD POPS: Prepare instant chocolate pudding according to package directions. Stir in ½ cup miniature marshmallows, ¼ cup semisweet chocolate chips, and ¼ cup chopped nuts (peanuts or walnuts). Pour into pop molds. Freeze.

BUTTERSCOTCH POPS: Prepare instant butterscotch pudding according to package directions, substituting root beer for milk in recipe. Pour into pop molds. Freeze.

TOFFEE POPS: Prepare instant vanilla pudding according to package directions. Stir in ½ cup chopped chocolate-covered toffee bars. Pour into pop molds. Freeze.

FRUITY POPS: Stir one cup boiling water into 1 (4-serving size) package gelatin dessert and ¼ cup sugar. Stir until dissolved. Stir in 1 ½ cups cold water. and mix in fruit (if used). Pour into pop molds. Freeze.

SIMPLE FRUITY POP VARIATIONS:
Strawberry: use strawberry gelatin with 1 cup pureed strawberries.

Lemonade: use lemon gelatin and ¼ cup lemon juice.

Watermelon: use watermelon gelatin and 1 cup pureed watermelon (seeds removed)

Orange Cream: use orange gelatin and 1 cup evaporated milk in place of water.

Use your imagination! Freezer pops made with gelatin desserts don't drip as much as pops made from drink mixes.

YOGURT POPS: Mix together 2 cups plain yogurt, 1 cup milk, 1 cup mashed fruit (your choice: strawberries, peaches, applesauce, pineapple, or ⅓ cup frozen concentrate orange or grape juice, or 6 tablespoons jam or preserves), 1 tablespoon sugar, and ½ teaspoon vanilla. Blend until smooth. Pour into pop molds. Freeze.

Mix and Match Quiche

(4-6 servings)

To make crust:

2 cups leftover rice (white or brown)
1 egg, beaten
1 tsp. soy sauce

Mix together rice, egg and soy sauce. Spread evenly to cover bottom and sides of well-buttered quiche pan or pie plate. Bake crust at 350 F for 10 minutes. Remove from oven.

To make filling:
Vegetables and (or) meat...
Choose one or two to total,
1-½ to 2 cups, cooked or cut-up

Peas
Green beans
Broccoli
Spinach
Mixed vegetables
Celery
Green pepper
4 eggs, beaten
1 ½ cups milk, cream or half-n-half (whichever you prefer—nonfat works fine)
1 cup cheese, grated (whatever you have around—Swiss, Cheddar, Monterey Jack, Colby, Mozzarella—in any combination)
Salt and pepper to taste
Dash nutmeg or ground mace

Place vegetable and/or meat in bottom of crust.
Mix together eggs, milk, and spices. Pour over vegetable/meat. Top with cheese. Bake at 350 degrees for 45 -

50 minutes, or until knife inserted near center of pie comes out clean. Remove from oven and let sit 10 minutes before slicing.

You can use almost any leftover vegetables or meats in this recipe. If you have eggs, milk, cheese and rice, you can practically clean out your refrigerator right into your quiche pan. To make a beautifully mellow brown top crust, remember to add the cheese last.

Hint for Parents:

Many children don't seem to like quiche. I've found that what they are tasting is the unusual flavor of the Swiss cheese that's frequently used in quiche. If you replace Swiss cheese in quiche recipes with a combination of Monterey Jack and Cheddar, kids will eat it up—and even ask for seconds!

Mix and Match
Quick Bread
(Makes two loaves or 12 muffins)

You can make muffins or loaves with this recipe.

3 cups flour
1 tsp salt
3 tsp cinnamon
½ tsp baking powder
1 tsp baking soda
2 eggs
1 cup oil
2 cups sugar
2 cups **MIX-N-MATCH** (see below)
3 tsp vanilla
1 cup chopped nuts or seeds (your choice)

MIX-N-MATCH...one or more of the following to equal two cups

Apples, grated or chopped
Applesauce
Apricots, chopped
Bananas, mashed or chopped
Berries
Carrots, cooked and mashed or grated
Dates or figs, pitted and finely chopped
Pears, fresh or canned, chopped
Pineapple, crushed and well-drained
Sweet Potatoes or Yams, cooked and mashed
Zucchini, grated and well-drained

Preparation:

Sift together dry ingredients. In separate bowl, beat eggs; add oil and sugar; cream together. Stir in vanilla and your choice of Mix-N-Match. Add dry ingredients; mix well. Stir in nuts (optional.) Spoon into two well-greased loaf pans. Bake at 325 degrees for 1 hour. If making muffins, bake at 375 degrees for 15 minutes.

Tasty Mix-N-Match Combos...

Carrot-Raisin-Walnut
Pumpkin-Raisin-Sunflower Seed
Apple-Cranberry-Walnut
Cranberry-Orange-Walnut

Fruit Grunt

(makes one loaf)

Any fresh fruit
Any flavor Jiffy™-boxed cake mix
Sugar

Generously butter a bread loaf pan. Place fruit in the bottom. Sprinkle with sugar. Prepare cake mix as directed and then pour over fruit in bread pan. Bake as directed on the box. Let cool and then invert to unmold. Serve warm with whipped cream.

A dab-of-this and a dab-of-that dip

(makes 2 cups)

In medium bowl, stir together:

1 pint sour cream
1 dry package Italian dressing mix
-or- 1 package dry Ranch-style
dressing mix
-or- 1 package dry onion soup mix
Serve "as is" or stir in your choice of the following items.
Serve cold with chips or chopped vegetables.

Add one item,
or mix together a combination of several:

1 small jar artichoke hearts (marinated), chopped
¼ cup bacon bits
¼ cup bell peppers, finely diced
¼ cup celery, finely diced
1 cup cheese, shredded (your choice)
2 tbsp. chilies (canned), chopped
1 small can crab meat, chopped
¼ cup olives, chopped (black or green)
¼ cup green onion, chopped or thinly sliced
½ cup roasted red peppers, finely chopped
1 cup salsa, chunky
½ cup smoked salmon, chopped
1 cup tomatoes (fresh), seeded and diced
½ cup water chestnuts, finely chopped

A Well-Stocked
Pantry is a Girl's Best Friend

Mix and Match Recipes can be used with so many of the regular items we all have hiding in our cupboards. But if you find you're using this style of cooking frequently, the following is a list of items helpful to keep on hand.

PANTRY ITEMS:

basil
bay leaves
beans, canned (black, kidney, pinto, white, and lentils)
beef broth, canned
bouillon cubes or granules (chicken and beef)
bread crumbs
catsup
cayenne
chicken, canned
chicken broth, canned
chili powder
cumin
egg noodles
flour
fruit, canned (peaches, pears, oranges, applesauce, mixed fruit)
garlic
garlic salt
ginger
herb blend
mushrooms, canned
mustard (dry, regular and Dijon-style)
nuts (walnuts, almonds, pecans)
oatmeal

olive oil
olives (black and green)
onion powder
oregano
Parmesan cheese
parsley flakes
pastas, assorted dry (spaghetti, fettuccine, manicotti, macaroni, seashells, bow-ties, penne)
pepper
raisins
rice (brown, white, long-grain)
sage
salt
soup, canned (tomato, chicken noodle, French onion, cream of mushroom, cream of chicken, cream of broccoli, whatever else your family likes)
soup, dry mixes (chicken noodle, French onion)
soy sauce
spaghetti sauce, jars or cans
sugar (white, brown, powdered)

taco seasoning packets
tomato paste
tomato sauce
tomatoes, crushed or diced
tomatoes, stewed (regular, Italian-style and Mexican-style)
thyme
tuna
vanilla extract
vegetables, assorted canned
vegetable oil
vegetable broth, canned
water chestnuts
Worcestershire sauce

REFRIGERATOR AND FREEZER SUPPLIES:
cheeses (cheddar, Monterey Jack, mozzarella, Parmesan, ricotta, Romano, Swiss)
corn kernels (canned)
cream cheese
eggs
ground beef (store in 1-pound packages in freezer)
margarine
milk
mixed vegetables, frozen
peas, frozen
sour cream
carrots
celery
green onions
peppers (green, red, yellow)
onions
parsley, fresh
potatoes
tofu

Choose-Your-Way Chicken

(6 servings)

½ cup flour
1 teaspoon paprika
½ teaspoon salt
½ teaspoon pepper
1 (3-lb.) chicken, cut up
Vegetable Oil

Heat oil in a skillet with a tight-fitting cover (for later) over medium-high heat. Add chicken and cook until brown on all sides, about 10 minutes. Reduce heat, cover and simmer for about 30-35 minutes, turning occasionally. Remove cover for last five minutes of cooking to crisp the chicken.

Breaded Chicken

Roll chicken in flour mixture, then beat one egg and dip chicken into egg. Next, mix 1 cup dry bread crumbs with ¼ teaspoon salt and roll chicken in mixture. Cook as above.

Super-Crunchy Chicken

Replace the flour in the above recipe with ¾ cup of crushed cornflakes. Melt enough margarine or butter in a bowl to dip chicken and then dredge in mixture. Cook as above.

Mix and Match
Cookies

(makes 2 dozen cookies)

Choose one box of cake mix...

Chocolate
Devil's Food
White
Yellow
Or other cake mix of your choice

Add...

2 eggs
½ cup vegetable oil

Stir in ½ to 1 cup of any of the following: (choose one or two)

Chocolate chips
Butterscotch chips
Peanut butter chips
Walnuts
Pecans
Almonds
Raisins
Dates
Dried cranberries
Dried cherries
Dried apricots or peaches, diced

In medium mixing bowl, stir together: cake mix, eggs, oil and any extra added ingredient. Drop by rounded teaspoons onto ungreased cookie sheet. Bake at 350 degrees for 10 minutes.

Mix and Match Your Way to a More Relaxing Day...

Spa Milk Bath

2 cups salt
2 cups baking soda
2 cups nonfat dry milk
Mix ingredients together. Store in airtight container.   To use, add one cup to warm bath water.

Facial Mask

1 cup finely chopped oatmeal (whirl in the blender briefly)
1 container live-culture plain (non-flavored) yogurt
½ cup lemon juice
Mix oatmeal with yogurt; stir in lemon juice. Apply to clean, dry skin on face and neck. Leave on skin for 15 to 20 minutes. Rinse with warm water. Pat dry.

Fizzing Bath Bombs

2 tablespoons cornstarch
2 tablespoons citric acid (sold as Fruit Fresh in the US)
¼ cup baking soda
3 tablespoon coconut oil
½ teaspoon fragrance oil (your choice)
In bowl, mix together cornstarch, citric acid and baking soda. Melt coconut oil and add fragrance. Slowly drizzle oils into powder mixture. Mix well. Scoop out by scant ¼ cup, roll into balls. Let sit for 2 - 3 hours, checking frequently to see if the balls have lost their shape. Reshape if necessary. Let dry for 48 hours. Wrap in clear plastic wrap, or colored wrap for gift giving. To use, just place in bath as water fills tub.

More Creative Cookies

(makes 3 dozen)

This master recipe makes four scrumptious cookie varieties—from one easy recipe!

Butter Cookies

Ingredients:
1 cup butter, softened
1 egg
2 cups all purpose flour
1 cup sugar
1 tablespoon vanilla extract
¼ teaspoon salt

We're cooking now:

Preheat oven to 350 degrees. Cream together butter and sugar until light and fluffy. Add egg; beat well. Blend in vanilla. Combine flour and salt; add to creamed mixture. Drop by rounded teaspoonfuls onto ungreased cookie sheets. Bake 10-12 minutes, or until golden brown.

These cookies are simple to make and easy to alter to make the three varieties on the following page.

Chocolate Mint Delights

Prepare Butter Cookie recipe adding 1 teaspoon mint extract with the vanilla. Add ½ cup cocoa with the flour and salt. Cream mixture and stir in 2/3 cup chocolate chips. Continue as in Butter Cookie recipe.

Lemon Ginger Cookies

Prepare Butter Cookie recipe substituting 2 teaspoon lemon extract for the vanilla. Add 2 teaspoons ground ginger with the flour and salt. Cream mixture. Roll dough into 1-inch balls. Place on ungreased cookies sheets. Flatten cookie dough with bottom of a glass into 2-inch circles. Bake 10-12 minutes. Sprinkle baked cookies with powdered sugar.

Almond Cranberry Cookies

Prepare Butter Cookie recipe adding 1 teaspoon almond extract with the vanilla. After creaming mixture, stir in ½ cup dried cranberries and ½ cup chopped toasted almonds. Continue as in Butter Cookie recipe.

Mix & Match Skillet Meal

(6 servings)

Choose ONE food from EACH of the following groups:

Breads and Cereals... Choose 1 cup raw

Macaroni	Bulgar
Spaghetti	Noodles
Rice (white or brown)	Any pasta

Sauce...(1 can soup plus 1½ cups milk, broth or water)

Cream of Potato	French Onion Soup
Cream of Chicken	Tomato Soup
Cream of Mushroom	Cream of Celery

Protein... (1 pound or 1½ cups cooked)

Chopped beef	Kielbasa
Chopped pork or ham	Frankfurters
Ground beef or turkey	Cooked dry beans
Chicken	Mackerel
Turkey	Salmon
Tuna	

Vegetables... (1½ to 2 cups canned, cooked or raw)

Carrots	Green beans
Peas	Green Pepper
Corn	Celery
Lima beans	Mixed vegetables
Broccoli	Spinach

Last, but not least...

½ to 1 cup cheese (any kind) can be stirred into sauce at the end of the cooking time.

We're Cooking Now...

Choose one food from each of the four groups above. Stir together in skillet. Season to taste with salt, pepper, soy sauce, onion flakes, garlic, or whatever spices you enjoy. Bring to a boil.

Reduce heat to lowest setting. Cover pan and simmer 30 minutes until pasta or rice is tender. Stir occasionally to prevent rice and pasta from sticking. Stir in cheese, if desired. Serve.

To bake in oven...

Mix all ingredients in casserole dish and cover tightly. Bake at 350 degrees for about 1 hour.

Our family's favorite Skillet Meal:
INTERNATIONAL SAUSAGE SKILLET
(6 servings)

½ - 1 pound Kielbasa (halved lengthwise and sliced thinly)
8 ounces dry pasta (twists, shells or Penne)
1 16-ounce can Italian Stewed Tomatoes (cut up, do NOT drain)
1 can French Onion Soup

In skillet, brown Kielbasa slices. Then prepare meal per instructions above.

Enlist Help in the Kitchen

One of the most important aspects of my household clean up and daily maintenance has been developing job titles for certain groups of chores. The job titles come complete with full job descriptions. Each child is given a particular task and then the jobs are rotated each week. A younger child will work more closely with a parent to accomplish these duties, but an older child or teen will often be able to handle the jobs by themselves.

Here are three examples of possible job titles and descriptions—these are probably the most important job titles that you'll want to assign each week. Be sure to create the same number of jobs as you have children so everyone has an assignment.

ASSISTANT COOK: Helps at each meal every day, helps the parent cook and prepare meals, learns to cook, does whatever they're capable of handling on their own, sets the table.

CLEAN UP CREW: Hand washes whatever needs to be hand washed (pots, pans, china), loads and runs the dishwasher, washes tables, cleans off stove and countertops, sweeps kitchen, sweeps or vacuums dining room floor.

RECYCLER/GARBAGE COLLECTOR: Empties all small garbage cans and waste baskets, cleans around cans, separates recycling (tin cans, aluminum, empty milk jugs, newspapers, laundry cartons, cardboard).

Warm and Wonderful Drink Mixes

Cafe Vienna Coffee Mix

½ cup instant coffee (regular or decaf)
1 cup powdered sugar
⅔ cup nonfat dry milk
½ teaspoon cinnamon
Use 2 heaping teaspoons per cup of hot water.

Fireside Coffee Mix

2 cups nondairy coffee creamer
1 ½ cups hot cocoa mix
1 ½ cups instant coffee (regular
        or decaf)
1 ½ cups powdered sugar
1 teaspoon ground cinnamon
½ teaspoon ground nutmeg
Combine all ingredients in large

bowl, stirring well. Store in airtight container. To make one cup, spoon two heaping tablespoons of mix into coffee mug. Add one cup boiling water, stir until well blended.

Russian Tea

1 cup instant tea, plain
1 cup Tang™
½ cup instant lemonade
1 teaspoon ground cloves
1 teaspoon cinnamon

...or...

Diet Russian Tea

1 cup low-cal Iced Tea Mix, with lemon
½ cup Tang™
1 teaspoon ground cloves
1 teaspoon cinnamon

Preparation for Both

Mix all ingredients and store in an airtight container. Dissolve 2-3 tablespoons per mug of boiling water to make a relaxing, spiced-fruity-tea drink. Proportions or tea, Tang and lemonade can be altered to your taste preference.

Super Smoothies

(Makes 1)

In the container of your blender or food processor, add:
1 scoop protein powder
1 cup small (or broken) ice cubes

Mix-N-Match Liquid ...Choose one, ½ cup

Fruit juice (orange, apple, pineapple--whatever your fancy)
Milk
Soy milk
Yogurt (any kind) Stir in ⅓ cup milk or water if it's thick.

Mix-N-Match Fruit: (fresh, frozen* or canned**) choose one or two, 1 cup total

Strawberries
Bananas (old brown ones work well for this)
Blueberries
Raspberries
Blackberries
Orange slices, peeled
Peaches
Pears
Pineapple
Fruit cocktail
Or anything else that strikes your fancy

If you use frozen fruit, don't thaw. Also, delete the ice from this recipe.

**If using canned fruit, use some of the juice in place of some (or all) of the liquid.*

Mix-N-Match Sweetener...
Choose One, ¼ to 1 teaspoon

Honey
Vanilla Extract
Almond Extract
Sugar
Stevia*
Or whatever sweetener you regularly use

Found at natural food stores. Use sparingly.

Mix It Up...

To prepare your Smoothie, put selected ingredient in blender, cover and process until smooth. Enjoy!

Cream-of-Anything Soup

(makes 1½ cups soup per person when reconstituted)

Ingredients:

2 cups dry instant milk
1 ¼ cups cornstarch--or--2 ½ cups flour
1 teaspoon pepper
1 teaspoon salt

Preparation:

Mix all ingredients together in a medium bowl. Store in a tightly covered container. To make into soup, use ⅓ cup of the cornstarch mix to 1 ¼ cups water--OR--½ cup of the flour mix to 1 ¼ cups water. Stir soup mix and water together in saucepan. Bring to a boil over medium heat, stirring constantly, until thickened.

Transform:

Then simply transform the soup using one of the following:

White Sauce - Use "as is"
Cream of Chicken - Add 1-2 teaspoons of chicken bouillon powder
Cream of Broccoli - Add 1 cup steamed broccoli
Cream of Mushroom - Add 1 cup sautéed mushrooms
Cream of Celery - Add 1 cup cooked celery
Cheese Sauce- Add one cup grated cheddar cheese
Cheesy Broccoli - Add ½ cup cooked broccoli plus ½ cup cheese

Top 10 Tips for Grocery Savings

Groceries are one of the few flexible items in a family's budget, but it can sometimes be challenging to find creative ways to save on regular family food costs. The following are some simple tips for reducing your grocery expenses. If you're an "old pro" at frugal living, some of these may be old hat, but I'm amazed at how many people still find these tips helpful. Here are my personal top 10 tried-and-true tactics for savings.

1) Plan your meals around items you already have on hand, and around the sale flyers from your local grocery stores. But be warned: Moderation in all things. One time I found ground turkey on sale for four pounds for a dollar. Well, being the good little frugal person that I am, I bought forty pounds. FORTY pounds?! Yikes! Do you have any idea how sick and tired my family got of ground turkey? I tried sneaking it into spaghetti sauce, casseroles, meat balls, you name it. Before they'd take a bite, someone in the family would always ask (with their nose crinkled up funny), "Is it TURKEY, Mom?" Now please understand—my family likes ground turkey—in moderation. But too much of a good thing is ... well, too much of a good thing.

2) Shop with cash. This is a surprisingly effective means of staying on budget. Somehow writing a check seems less "concrete" than paying cash, making it easier to spend more than intended.

3) Keep a Price Diary. List all regularly purchased items (food, toiletries, paper products, etc.) in a small notebook that easily slips into your purse or pocket when you go shopping. When you're browsing through store advertisements or doing your actual shopping, write down (in pencil!) the lowest price you see for each item listed in your Price Diary (change the prices when you see lower prices than you've already written in the notebook). This way you'll know for sure if a sale price is low enough to make it worth stocking up.

4) A simple rule of thumb when you're shopping is: "Look high, look low." Stores often place the most expensive items at eye level. Don't be embarrassed to crawl around on your hands and knees in the grocery store looking for bargains. You might get some funny looks from other shoppers, but the cashiers will be amazed at how much food you're buying for so little money. And the look of approval you'll give yourself in the mirror when you've stayed within your budget is worth a few laughs at the store, believe me!

5) Sometimes a store will offer what's known as Loss Leaders — those items the store will sell so cheaply, they'll actually take a loss on each sale. They're hoping to entice new customers into the store who will then purchase other items in addition to the sale item. You need to hold strong against impulse purchases in these situations. Just run into the store, buy the Loss Leaders, don't do ANY browsing, and get out of there FAST before temptation strikes — or you may find your best laid money-saving plans waylaid by cute little floral arrangements for the upcoming holiday.

6) One simple approach to meal planning is setting a price goal for each meal. For example: Breakfast = $0.50 per person, Dinner = $3 - $4 total.

7) Check store entrances or bulletin boards for special flyers, and don't forget to look in local newspapers for additional coupons.

8) For the healthiest and freshest foods, shop the perimeter of the store. Dairy, meat, and produce departments are usually located around the outer walls, while you'll find all those fancy prepackaged "food" items (and I use the term "food" lightly) located in the center of the store. Avoid going down these aisles ... these are not only less healthy spots for buying "food" but they're also the location of many impulse buys. (Did you REALLY need that box of chocolate-covered frozen cream puffs? If you'd stayed on the perimeter, you wouldn't have even seen the chemical-filled snack foods.

9) Natural food co-ops are becoming quite common. This can be a great way to purchase organic fruits and vege-tables, whole grains and other usually expensive items at competitive prices.

10) Cook in bulk. Those of you who have read *Frozen Assets*, know that I have found incredible ways to save money by bulk cooking for the freezer. Over a five-year period, I was able to save $24,000 on my grocery bills. Bulk cooking involves the preparation of many meals in a single cooking ses-sion. It allows you the opportunity to take advan-tage of large sale items, bulk pricing and avoidance of takeout, since you always have a dinner "ready in the freezer."

Mix and Match Fruit Crisp

(makes 6 servings)

Ingredients:

2 cans pie filling (your choice: cherry, apply, berry)
1 can crushed pineapple
1 cup pecans or walnuts (optional)
1 box yellow cake mix
1 stick butter or margarine, melted

Preparation:

Mix together pie filling and pineapple. Pour into a 13 x 9-inch baking pan. Sprinkle nuts (if used) on top of filling. Dump the cake mix directly out of the box onto the filling and nuts mixture. Press lightly to make a smooth top over the filling. Evenly pour melted butter over top of cake mix (spread gently to cover). Bake at 350 degrees for 30-40 minutes or until the cake top is golden brown (may still be a bit soft, but will form more of a crust as it cools). Cool for 10 minutes. Serve warm or cold. Top with ice cream or whipped topping, if desired.

Mix and Match Fried Rice

(6 servings)

Ingredients:

12 ounces regular long grain white rice
1 ½ tablespoons plus 2 teaspoons oriental sesame oil
1 ½ cup onion, finely chopped
2 teaspoons fresh ginger root, pared and minced
3 teaspoons minced garlic
☐ teaspoon red pepper flakes, crushed
2 eggs, beaten
5 tablespoons soy sauce

Mix-N-Match
Veggies...Choose 2 or 3

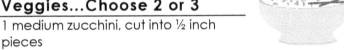

1 medium zucchini, cut into ½ inch pieces
1 red, green or yellow bell pepper, coarsely chopped
1 cup snow peas, stem ends and veins removed, cut into 1 inch pieces
9 asparagus spears, cut into ½ inch pieces
1 cup broccoli, cut into small pieces
2 green onions, sliced
1 cup leeks, cut into thin strips
1 cup carrots, thinly sliced or diced
2 celery stalks, sliced thinly
½ cup unsalted peanuts, chopped coarsely

Mix-N-Match Protein...Choose 1

2 cups cooked chicken breasts, cut into ½ inch pieces
2 cups cooked turkey meat, cut into ½ inch pieces
2 cups cooked shrimp
2 cups cooked ham, diced
1 pound tofu, drained and cut into ½ inch pieces

Putting it all together...

Cook rice according to package directions. In large skillet or wok, sauté onion, ginger, garlic and pepper flakes in 1 ½ tablespoons sesame oil. Cook over medium-high heat for two minutes. Add your choice of Mix-N-Match vegetables. Cook, stirring frequently 3 to 4 minutes, until vegetables are just softened. Stir in your choice of Mix-N-Match cooked meat and continue cooking until heated through. In a separate pan, scramble eggs. Stir eggs and vegetable mixture into rice. Stir in soy sauce. Sauté in skillet for five minutes more with 2 teaspoons sesame oil; stir frequently. Serve hot.

Pick A Pocket

(Makes 1)

Choose one...

A soft flour tortilla (wheat or white flour, of course the wheat is better for you!)
or ½ of a pita pocket
or a slice or two of toasted bread

Fill or top with any of the following combinations for a quick and tasty meal or snack...
Turkey and Swiss Cheese
Turkey, Swiss Cheese and Spinach
Cheese and Broccoli
Ham and Swiss Cheese
Ham, Cheddar Cheese and Broccoli
Turkey breast and Mushrooms
Mushrooms, Swiss Cheese and Onions
Bacon, Lettuce and Tomato (had to include the ol' standby!)
Turkey, Lettuce and Tomato
Grilled Chicken breast, Mushrooms and Swiss cheese

See how many combos you can come up with! It's always great to have a bag of flour tortillas on hand for these quick rolls up. Simply toss the tortilla on a plate, add toppings, zap in the microwave for 30 seconds (if desired) and you have a quick and easy lunch (or dinner) that didn't come from a box!
from The Rush Hour Cook Series ~ www.championpress.com

Mix-n-Match
MEATBALL MANIA!

Cooking up a large batch of meatballs in advance to store in the freezer goes a long way toward establishing a supply of quick and easy meals. And if you take advantages of sales on ground beef and stock up, this can be a tremendous boon to your family budget, too!

In addition to stirring meatballs into spaghetti sauce, you can also use them in soups, serve them on skewers (kids love this!), or heat in brown gravy or a warmed can of cream of mushroom soup served with mashed potatoes.

The following recipes prepare a large batch of freezer meatballs and also include examples of ways to use frozen meatballs. The sauces require some preparation, but the meals go together quickly with your stockpile of precooked meatballs waiting in the freezer.

MILLIONS of MEATBALLS

(this makes a lot—at least four dozen, depending on size)
12-ounces tomato sauce
1 ½ cups dry bread crumbs
4 eggs, lightly beaten
½ cup onion, finely chopped
¼ cup green pepper, finely chopped
1 teaspoons salt, optional
⅓ teaspoon dried thyme, crushed
⅓ teaspoon dried marjoram, crushed
4 pounds ground beef

In a large mixing bowl, combine first eight ingredients. Add ground beef and mix well. Shape into meatballs (use a small cookie scoop if available) and place on boiler pan so grease can drain while cooking. Bake uncovered in 350 degree oven for 30 minutes. Divide into meal-sized portions. To prevent from freezing into a solid meatball-mass, freeze individually on cookie sheets and then place in freezer bags. Label and freeze.

To serve meatballs, thaw completely and reheat with your choice of sauces (six sample sauce recipes follow).

SWEET-N-SOUR MEATBALLS
(5 servings)

1 (14-oz) can pineapple tidbits or chunks, un-drained
¼ cup brown sugar
2 tablespoons cornstarch
½ cup water
¼ cup cider vinegar
1 teaspoon soy sauce (or more to taste)
1 family meal-sized portion of freezer meatballs
1 (5-oz) can water chestnuts, drained and thinly sliced
1 green pepper, cut in strips

Drain pineapple tidbits, reserving syrup. In medium saucepan, combine brown sugar and cornstarch. Blend in reserved syrup, water, cider vinegar and soy sauce. Cook and stir over low heat until thick and bubbly. Carefully stir in meatballs, water chestnuts, green pepper strips and pineapple. Heat to boiling. Serve over hot cooked rice.

CHILI-DAY MEATBALLS
(5 servings)

This recipe sounds a little strange (chili sauce and grape jelly?), but it tastes like burgundy sauce (only without the wine)
1 (12-ounce) jar chili sauce
1 (1-ounce) jar grape jelly
2 tablespoons lemon juice
1 cube beef bouillon dissolved in ½ cup water
1 family meal-sized portion of freezer meatballs

Whisk together chili sauce, grape jelly, lemon juice and bouillon, breaking up all clumps. Simmer on low heat until sauce starts to thicken. Add freezer meatballs; cook in sauce until meatballs are fully thawed and heated through. Serve over hot cooked noodles or rice.

MEATBALL SANDWICHES
(6 servings)

1 family meal-sized portion of freezer meatballs (approximately 4-5 meatballs per person)
6 hot dog buns (or hoagie rolls)
6 thin slices mozzarella cheese
2 cups prepared spaghetti sauce

Thaw meatballs and spaghetti sauce (if using frozen). Place both in medium saucepan and heat thoroughly. Place the heated meatballs into warmed buns. Ladle small amounts of spaghetti sauce onto each sandwich; place mozzarella slice onto each sandwich.

TOMATO-SAUCED MEATBALLS
(5 servings)

1 (10 ¾-oz) can condensed tomato soup
½ cup water
1 teaspoon Worcestershire sauce
1 family meal-sized portion of freezer meatballs

Mix together soup, water and Worcestershire sauce. Place meatballs in a medium sized saucepan; pour soup mixture over meatballs. Simmer until meatballs are heated through. Serve over hot cooked rice.

MEATBALLS STROGANOFF
(5 servings)

1 (10 ¾-oz) can condensed cream of mushroom
      soup
½ cup sour cream or plain yogurt
1 cup mushrooms, sliced and cooked in butter until
      soft
1 family meal-sized portion of freezer meatballs

In medium saucepan, mix together mushroom soup and sour cream. Gently stir in mushrooms and meatballs. Simmer until meatballs are heated through. Serve over hot cooked rice or over egg noodles tossed with melted butter and chopped parsley.

CATALINA MEATBALLS
(5 servings)

1 medium onion, thinly sliced
2 teaspoons olive oil
1 bottle Catalina salad dressing
1 family meal-sized portion of freezer meatballs

Sauté onion slices in olive oil until softened. Place frozen meatballs in medium skillet. Pour dressing over meatballs. Cover skillet and cook over low heat until dressing caramelizes on meatballs and onion, and the meatballs are fully thawed and heated through. Serve over rice.

Meal in a Muffin

(makes 1 dozen)

Choose one from each of the following:

Protein...1 cup cooked

Tuna
Ground beef, pork or turkey
Ham, cubed
Chopped beef, pork or ham
Chicken
Turkey
Fish
Frankfurters

Vegetable... ½ cup cooked

Carrots
Green beans
Onion
Corn
Peas
Broccoli
Spinach
Mixed Vegetables

Other ingredients:

1 package refrigerator biscuits
2 eggs, lightly beaten
Shredded cheese for garnish, optional

Preparation:

Open the biscuits and separate them. Roll or press each biscuit into a 4-inch wide circle. Place into ungreased muffin tins, spreading across bottom and up the sides of each muffin well to form a small cup (it doesn't have to fill the entire muffin--they will expand as they cook). In a mixing bowl, stir together eggs, meat and vegetables. Spoon one heaping tablespoon of filling into each biscuit cup, top with small amount of cheese (if used), and bake at 350 degrees until the filling is set (15-18 minutes). Serve hot. These can be frozen ahead of time and reheated in the microwave, or served at room temperature for a snack.

You could also use this recipe to make mini-muffins for a creative appetizer.

Mom's Magic Seasoning

Take all your "dibs and dabs" of leftover spices and combine them ALL together. Mix and store in a cute little crock or jar. You now have your own one-of-a-kind, all purpose seasoning. Tastes great on grilled meats, salads, flavored vinegars, spaghetti sauce...anything that needs a "touch of magic."

You can also use your seasoning to create a Magic Snack Mix. Simply toss a bag of oyster crackers with melted butter and Mom's Magic Seasoning. Store in a cookie jar.

Champion Chili

(8 generous servings)

2 pounds lean ground beef
2 cans (14.5-ounce) Mexican-style stewed tomatoes
1 tablespoon sugar
1 small can tomato paste
½ teaspoon cumin
¼ teaspoon salt

Choose as many as you like:

1 cup onion, chopped
2 cloves minced garlic
1 can corn
1 (14.5-ounce) can kidney beans
1 can garbanzo beans
1 tablespoon red pepper flakes
⅓ cup jalapenos
     (include the juice if you like it really hot!)
1 red bell pepper, chopped
1 green pepper, chopped
3 tablespoons chili powder
1 tablespoon oregano
1 tablespoon basil leaves
1 tablespoon Cajun spice mix

Choose one:

1 cup red wine
1 bottle of beer
1 cup of coffee
1 cup beef broth

Choose one "secret" ingredient...

1 tablespoon brown sugar
1 tablespoon Worcestershire
3 Hershey Kisses or 2 tbsp. chocolate chips (to melt in)
1 tablespoon cocoa
1 teaspoon instant coffee
¼ teaspoon cinnamon

Choose one (or none!)

Instant white rice
Elbow macaroni

Sauté meat in a large skillet over medium heat until brown. Drain. If you have chosen garlic and/or onion, add them to the meat and cook another minute or two. Add all other ingredients you have chosen, stirring well. Cook on medium heat for 5-10 minutes and then reduce heat to low for at least 40 minutes. Of course, as with most soups, stews and chili recipes--the longer they cook, the more the flavors meld! For great tasting flavor, try putting this recipe together in the morning and then leaving it in a slow cooker on a low setting for a great dinner meal. If desired, prepare rice or macaroni in a separate pot. Mix into chili prior to serving, or place in bottom of individual bowls and pour the chili over the pasta or rice. Have a selection of your favorite toppings and garnishes on hand, so everyone can "customize" their own serving to their own taste.

Perfect Parfaits
(makes one)

Choose ⅔ cup of any of the following fresh fruits: cantaloupe, honeydew, watermelon, oranges, pineapple, kiwi, berries, apples, bananas

¼ to ½ cup nonfat plain, vanilla or
lemon-flavored yogurt
⅓ cup granola

Place ⅓ of the fruit in a tall glass. Top with a thin layer of yogurt and then granola. Repeat the layers ending with the yogurt. Garnish with a few pieces of fruit. Vanilla pudding can also be used in place of yogurt.

Quick & Easy Kids Bake
(6-8 servings)

1 jar spaghetti sauce
grated Parmesan cheese (if desired)

Choose one....

1 package penne
1 package rigatoni
1 package egg noodles
1 package elbow macaroni

Choose one...

1 lb. ground chuck or beef
1 lb. ground turkey

Choose one or two...

1 cup mozzarella cheese
1 cup cheddar cheese
1 cup ricotta cheese
1 cup cottage cheese
½ cup sour cream

Preheat oven to 350 degrees. Cook noodles according to package directions. Brown your choice of meat in a skillet over medium heat. Drain. Add jar of spaghetti sauce to meat and stir. Mix your choice of cheese together in a small bowl. Place pasta, meat and cheese mixture in a lightly sprayed casserole dish. Bake in oven for 30 minutes or until heated through. Top with Parmesan cheese, if desired.

Suggestions for Using Leftovers:

~ Bread (loaf ends, slices starting to dry): bread pudding, French toast, meat loaf extender, croutons, stuffing, bread crumbs

~ Eggs (hard-cooked): casseroles, salads, sandwiches

~ Fruit (fresh, canned or frozen): smoothies, milk shakes, gelatin desserts, cobblers, muffins, fruit bread, jam, freezer pops, sauces

~ Meats, poultry, or fish (cooked): soups, stew, salad, quiche, enchiladas, stir fry, sandwiches, pot pies

~ Potatoes (cooked): pot pie, salads, soups, stew, potato patties

~ Rice, pasta (cooked): casseroles, soups, puddings

~ Vegetables (cooked): casseroles, quiche, salads, soups, topping on baked potato, pot pies

One of the things we do with our leftovers is to prepare a Party Tray meal. I'll take all the collected leftovers out of the fridge and freezer, reheat them and then spread them out buffet style. When I first tried this, I was amazed at what a success it was with our family. It made having leftovers fun—instead of a chore!

Sauté A Side Dish:

Buttered Bananas

1 banana per person
brown sugar
butter

Gently sauté whole, firm bananas in butter. Cook uncovered until tender—not mushy. Melt brown sugar into the bananas at the end, being careful not to scorch.

Caramelized Apples

1 apple per person
brown sugar
butter

On stovetop, melt butter in a Pyrex style baking dish. Add peeled, sliced apples in a single layer, turning to coat. Sprinkle with a few tablespoons of brown sugar. Cover and gently simmer until fork tender and glazed with melted sugar, being careful not to overcook. 10 minutes should be the maximum.

Glazed Carrots

6 servings

1 large package fresh carrots
3-4 tablespoons butter
2 tablespoons brown sugar

Cut fresh, peeled carrots into julienne strips. Simmer in pan of water till just fork tender. Drain. Melt in the butter and brown sugar to coat and glaze the carrots. Blend and stir until well-glazed, being careful not to scorch, cooking for just a minute or so longer.

Plenty of Pies

(6-8 servings per pie)

Start with a dark chocolate cookie crust, prepared and cooled. Then choose from the following...

Caramel Craze Pie

turtle ice cream softened
caramel sauce on top and whipped cream

Chocolate Mint

mint chip ice cream
chocolate sauce drizzled to decorate

Coffee-Lovers

coffee ice cream
shaved chocolate (use a potato peeler and Hershey bar)
crumbled on top, or crumble a Heath or Skor bar

Cookies & Cream Supreme

Cookies and cream ice cream
top with crumbled Oreo Cookies
drizzle with chocolate sauce for a finishing flair

Soften the ice cream enough to fill the pie shell. Refreeze until serving time.

Quick Fix
Baking Mix

4 cups all-purpose flour
4 cups whole wheat flour*
1 ⅓ cup nonfat dry milk
¼ cup baking powder
1 teaspoon salt
1 ½ cups vegetable shortening or margarine (don't use oil)

In large mixing bowl, stir dry ingredients together until well-mixed. Cut in shortening or margarine until well-mixed. Store in closed, covered container. If stored in pantry, use within one month; or store in refrigerator.

NOTE: If margarine is used, store baking mix in refrigerator only—the margarine will go rancid if stored at room temperature for any length of time. Stir lightly before use.

*All-purpose flour, cornmeal, or rolled oats can be substituted for the whole wheat flour.

Mix and Match Mix
~ Quick Fixes ~

Biscuits

(Makes 20 two-inch biscuits)
4 cups Baking Mix
  (see Quick Fix Baking Mix Recipe on Page 55)
1 cup water

Add water to baking mix and stir about 20 times. Turn dough onto lightly floured board. Knead 10-15 strokes. Roll or pat to ¾ inch thickness and cut with biscuit cutter. Bake on ungreased pan or cookie sheet in a 400 degree preheated oven for 12-15 minutes. To freeze, place in freezer bag.

Biscuit variations:
1. add ¼ cup bacon, cooked and minced
2. add ⅔ cup grated cheese and ½ teaspoon garlic powder
3. ⅔ cup raisins and 2 tablespoons sugar

Shortcake

(6 servings)

2 ⅓ cup Baking Mix
  (see Quick Fix Baking Mix Recipe on Page 55)
½ cup water
3 tablespoons sugar
3 tablespoons margarine or butter, melted

Stir ingredients until soft dough forms. Spread into two un-greased 8-inch square baking pans. Bake at 425 degrees for 15-20 minutes or until golden brown. Slice into squares. Serve with sliced berries and whipped cream.

For drop shortcake: after stirring, drop dough by ¼ cup amounts onto un-greased cookie sheets. Bake 10-12 minutes or until golden brown. Slice in half and serve with fruit and whipped topping.

Snack Cake

(6 servings)
Topping:
¼ cup flour
⅓ cup brown sugar
¼ teaspoon cinnamon
1½ tablespoons butter, softened

Cake:
1 ½ cups Baking Mix
     (see Quick Fix Baking
      Mix Recipe Page 55)
⅓ cup sugar
½ cup water
1 egg
½ teaspoon vanilla

Combine topping ingredients with pastry cutter or fork until crumbly; set aside. In large bowl, stir sugar into Baking Mix. In a separate bowl beat water, egg and vanilla until smooth and frothy. Stir egg mixture into Baking Mix; beat until smooth. Pour batter into greased 8x8 pan; sprinkle with topping. Bake at 350 degrees, for 25 minutes or until firm in the center. Makes a great coffee cake.

Dumplings

(makes 6-8 dumplings)
2 cups Baking Mix
(see Quick Fix Baking Mix Recipe on Page 55)
⅔ cup water

Stir together baking mix and water. Drop by heaping tablespoons into boiling soup or stew. Cook covered for 10- minutes, then remove lid and cook uncovered for an additional 10 minutes.

Just for Kids...
Recipes that
Guarantee Fun!

Sidewalk Chalk

Plaster of Paris
Warm water
Powdered tempera paint
Molds (small cardboard tubes, trays that manicotti come in, plastic candy molds, paper cups, cupcake liners, anything you can either pop the chalk out of or peel away from the finished chalk)

Mix the plaster of Paris according to package directions (using warm water). The consistency should be thick, but still pour-able. Add a small amount of powdered paint (if desired), and then pour into molds. Let harden 48 hours.

Soap Crayons

1 ¾ cups Ivory Snow™ powder
¼ cup water
50 drops food coloring
Ice cube tray (or plastic candy molds)

Mix together soap powder and
water. Add food coloring. Stir.
Pour mixture into ice cube tray. Allow crayons to harden.
Pop the crayons out of the tray and use to write in the
bathtub.

Homemade Stickers

Assorted paper pictures (cut from magazines)
Scissors
Small bowl
White glue
White vinegar
Paintbrush or cotton swabs
Wax paper

Combine two parts glue and one part vinegar in bowl. Stir
well. Brush a thin layer of glue mixture onto the back of
each cut out with a paint brush or cotton swab, making
sure to cover all the edges. Place the stickers on a sheet
of wax paper and allow to air dry completely, (about an
hour). Any flavor of powdered gelatin dessert, mixed with
a small amount of water can also be used for the "glue" to
paint on the back of the stickers. (Tastes great when licking
the stickers!)

Crazy Crayons

Crayons (unwrapped and broken into pieces)
Pan spray
Glass jars (baby food jars work well)
Saucepan
Metal muffin tin or plastic candy molds

If you're using muffin tins, place several crayon pieces directly into each hole of the muffin tin. You can make the new crayons all one color, or mix complimentary colors to add interest. Heat the muffin tin in a 325 degree oven for five minutes (or until crayon bits are melted). Check frequently. Cool. Pop out of muffin tins.

To make crayons in plastic candy molds, place several pieces of crayon into each jar. Spray the candy molds with pan spray. Place the glass jar into saucepan, adding enough water to the pan to cover the jar halfway. Heat the pan over low heat until the crayons have melted. Watch constantly. Carefully pour the melted crayon into the candy molds. Let the crayons cool and pop them out of the molds.

Craft Dough Recipe

2 cups flour
1 cup salt
1 cup cold water

Mix ingredients together and knead until it becomes a medium-stiff dough. Add more flour or water to adjust consistency if needed. To color, add several drops of food coloring and knead until mixed thoroughly. Store unused clay in sealed plastic bags in the refrigerator. Use as modeling clay, or roll out like cookie dough and cut with a cookie cutter. To make ornaments, bake on cookie sheet at 225 degrees for about one hour, or until it feels hard to the touch. Cool on wire rack. To protect your clay creations, dip in melted paraffin or coat with polyurethane.

Bubbles

5 cups water
½ cup liquid Joy™ dishwashing detergent
2 Tablespoons glycerin (found at drug stores)
Add dish soap and glycerin to pan of water. Stir gently to mix— don't let suds build up.

Edible Finger Paints

Mix up a box of vanilla instant pudding and divide it up into two to four smaller dishes. Use food coloring and color the pudding. Cover your kitchen table with waxed paper. You and your children can create wonderful designs and majestic artwork with the pudding on the waxed paper. When you're finished, lick your fingers and enjoy! Using the waxed paper makes clean up easy, too.

Clay Ornaments

⅓ cup water
½ cup salt
1 cup flour
food coloring
yarn or string
paint or varnish

Mix together water, salt and flour. Divide into sections. Add food coloring, if desired. Roll out on a floured board to about a ¼-inch thickness. Cut with cookie cutters. Use a pencil to put a hole in the top of each ornament, large enough to put yarn through for hanging. Place ornaments on baking sheet covered with foil. Bake at 275 degrees for one hour. Let cool and then paint or leave plain for a natural look. When done with decorating, let dry. Once dry, varnish the ornaments. Push yarn through the holes and hang.

Other books that may be of interest:

BY DEBORAH TAYLOR-HOUGH...
FROZEN ASSETS: HOW TO COOK FOR A DAY AND EAT FOR A MONTH... $14.95
FROZEN ASSETS LITE & EASY $19.95
A SIMPLE CHOICE: A PRACTICAL GUIDE FOR SAVING TIME, MONEY AND SANITY
COOKING FOR THE FREEZER (AUDIO TAPE)
LIVING WITHIN YOUR MEANS (AUDIO TAPE)

Other Champion Cookbooks:

CRAZY ABOUT CROCKPOTS:
101 EASY AND INEXPENSIVE RECIPES FOR LESS THAN $1 A SERVING

CRAZY ABOUT CROCKPOTS:
101 RECIPES FOR ENTERTAINING AT LESS THAN .75 A SERVING

CRAZY ABOUT CROCKPOTS: 101 RECIPES FOR SOUPS AND STEWS

HEALTHY FOODS: AN IRREVERENT GUIDE TO UNDERSTANDING
NUTRITION AND FEEDING YOUR FAMILY WELL

THE FRANTIC FAMILY COOKBOOK: (MOSTLY) HEALTHY MEALS IN MINUTES

THE RUSH HOUR COOK

365 QUICK, EASY & INEXPENSIVE DINNER MENUS

You can view samples, excerpts, and order at a special price when you visit our web site at www.championpress.com